Interce

Mini-Course

"Growing Personally
As An Intercessor"

Rev. Denny Finnegan

DEDICATION

There have been many who have encouraged me and taught me about Intercessory Prayer through the years, from friends to various authors. In particular, I wish to express my thanks to those Staff and Volunteers of Presbyterian Reformed Ministries International who have ministered to me since 1986. Because of their faithfulness to the Lord, continued confidence in how the Lord had gifted me, along with their encouragements to "fan into flame the gift(s) of God" which they sensed the Holy Spirit had placed within me, I was inspired to persevere in discovering, developing and deepening the call of ministry God has placed upon my life.

Rev. Denny Finnegan

PUBLISHED BY EXCELLENT PRESS
FROM EXCELLENT ADVENTURES!, INC
ATLANTA, GEORGIA, U.S.A
PRINTED IN THE U.S.A.

Excellent Press is a subsidiary of Excellent Adventures!, Inc. Excellent
Adventures!,Inc. is dedicated to serving the local church and missional
organizations. We believe God's vision for this division of Excellent
Adventures!, Inc. is to provide church leaders and pastors with biblical,
user-friendly materials that will help them evangelize, disciple and
minister to children, youth and families. We are also dedicated to
serving first time authors of Christian books and materials.

It is our prayer that this workbook from Excellent Press will help you
discover Biblical truths for your own life and help you meet the needs
of others. May God richly bless you.

For more information about Excellent Press, please contact Joe
Schlosser at 1-888-740-4834 or by email at joseph@schlosser.com

All scripture quotations, unless otherwise indicated, are taken from the
HOLY BIDLE, NEW

INTERNATIONAL VERSION (NIV) Copyright © 1973, 1978, 1984
by International Bible Society.

Used by permission of Zondervan. All rights reserved. Scripture
quotations marked NAU are taken from the New American Updated
Version of the Holy Bible.
ISBN: 978-0-9889584-3-2

Cover design and interior layout by Joe Schlosser.

CONTENTS

www.DennyFinnegan.com

ACKNOWLEDGMENTS

I would like to acknowledge the dedication and assistance of my wife Marcia, along with Presbyterian-Reformed Ministries International, The Dunamis Institute, and Excellent Press in making this mini-course workbook become a reality. To God be all the glory

INTRODUCTION

The purpose of this study is to help those who are sensing a *deeper call* for *Intercessory Prayer Training* and how to grow personally in Intercessory Prayer.

It is a follow-up to the 13 week small group study ***Prayer Ministry in the Local Church*** from the series *Foundations, Understanding Prayer Ministry* and is the first of three study guides on Intercessory Prayer, Healing Prayer, and Prophetic Prayer.

Why this study is divided into Two Sections

I believe that, in order to develop an intercessory prayer base in the local church *that lasts*, it is important to begin with the individual. You cannot grow prayer within the congregation, unless you first grow the hunger for prayer and the desire to intercede in the heart of the individual members. That is why the focus of this six-part Bible Study series is on developing the individual in intercessory prayer and is broken into two parts:

SECTION 1 lays a foundation with *Some Basics on Intercessory Prayer*;

SECTION 2 offers *An Intercessory Prayer Model*

But *growing prayer within the congregation* does not begin until it begins with you, personally!

~ *Pastor Denny Finnegan*

OVERVIEW OF LESSONS

SECTION 1: *"Basics on Intercessory Prayer"*

> **Lesson #1** - A Review of Our Purpose: "What Is Intercessory Prayer?"

> **Lesson #2** -The Foundation for All Our Ministry: "Intimacy with Jesus"

SECTION 2: *"An Intercessory Prayer Model"*

> **Lesson #3** - *Praying by Listening - Part 1*: - "Honoring God" and "Personal Cleansing

> **Lesson #4** - *Praying by Listening - Part 2*: "Dealing with the Enemy" and "Personal Concerns"

> **Lesson #5** - *Praying by Listening - Part 3*: - "Meditate on the Word" and "Pray What God Gives You"

> **Lesson #6** - *Praying by Listening - Part 4*: - "Persevering Prayer"

Study Tracks Overview:

The following is a suggested format for a Sunday School Class Setting. In a small group study setting, you can allow more time for each of the three areas *"as the Holy Spirit leads."*

1. Laying a Biblical Foundation - 30 minutes
2. Practicing What We Have Been Taught - 20 minutes
3. *"Praying for Vision"* - 10 minutes

SECTION 1: "BASICS ON INTERCESSORY PRAYER"

Lesson 1: A Review Of Our Process:

"What is Intercessory Prayer?"

Lesson 2: Foundations For All Our Ministry:

"Intimacy With Jesus

www.DennyFinnegan.com

LESSON 1: A Review of Our Process – "What is Intercessory Prayer?"

Laying a Biblical Foundation

Jesus Prepares the Way for Our Intercessions.

The word "to intercede" means to "intervene between parties with a view to reconciling differences; mediate" (Webster's New Collegiate Dictionary). When we do "intercessory prayer" we are choosing to speak on behalf of someone else to God, the Father, in the Name of Jesus, the Son, just as Jesus, the Son, speaks to the Father on our behalf.

As the writer of Hebrews 4:14-16 says:

"14 *Since then we have a great high priest who has passed through the heavens, Jesus the Son of God, let us hold fast our confession. 15 For we do not have a high priest who cannot sympathize with our weaknesses, but One who has been tempted in all things as we are, yet without sin. 16 Let us therefore draw near with confidence to the throne of grace, that we may receive mercy and may find grace to help in time of need."* (Hebrews 4:14-16)

Discussion:

1) How does Jesus *intercede* for us?

_____

_____

_____

_____

2) How can Jesus' work as our *"high priest who [can] sympathize with our weaknesses"* encourage us to pray for our own needs? for the needs of others?

_____

_____

_____

_____

Three *Different Ways* We Can *Intercede*

Because of Jesus, we can now approach God's throne of mercy and grace *boldly*: for ourselves and for others. When we intercede for someone else, we are choosing to serve them with our prayers, and with our requests so that God's mercy and grace are poured out upon them.

There are three particular ways that we might find ourselves acting on behalf of someone else with our prayer requests:

Personal Intercession: Praying alone, making petitions for ourselves or for someone else. We could be praying for one person or many people.

Event Intercession: Praying with one person, more than one person or many others, in a particular location. We could be praying for one person or many people.

Strategic Intercession: Praying with one person, more than one person or many others, in a particular location, with a particular awareness and sense of authority from the Lord to overcome any opposition set up against those for whom we pray. We could be praying for one person or many people.

Discussion:

1) Where have you seen these *three different types of intercession* take place?

_____

_____

_____

_____

_____

2) Have you ever participated in any of these *three different types of intercession*? If yes, give details?

_____

_____

_____

_____

3) What are some of your struggles about intercessory prayer? What are some of your struggles about any of these *three different types of intercession?*

_____

_____

_____

_____

_____

Practicing What We Have Been Taught

An Intercessory Prayer Model

If I were to try and summarize what "Intercessory Prayer" is like - what it is we might ask of God for someone - I would use Jesus' own words in response to one of His own followers who said, *"Lord, teach us to pray ..."* (Luke 11:1). In Matthew 6:9-13, Matthew records the more expanded version of Jesus' prayer in Luke 11. The key verse for me is Matthew 6:10, where Jesus teaches us to pray, *"Your kingdom come, Your will be done on earth as it is in heaven."* The phrase, *"Your will be done..."* could also be translated as, *"Your will be birthed..."*. And the verses that follow show specific ways that we are asking for God's will *"to be birthed"* in our lives, in the lives of others, and in our world.

God wants to use our prayers on behalf of others

8

"to birth His will" in the lives of others whether it be in our families, our communities or in nations around the world. The next three lessons will give you a general overview of how the Holy Spirit may call you and equip you to serve others *through prayer* with the mercy and grace of God found only in Jesus Christ.

Instructions:

1) Take each of the following phrases from the "Our Father", and ask God to show you *how* to pray it, and for *whom* to pray.

2) *You do not have to finish the whole prayer.* You have permission to stay with any verse as long as you want.

Let's Pray ...

Vs.9: *"Our Father in heaven, hallowed be Your Name,"* - Spend time thanking God, the Father, for *Who He is*, and for *what He has done*.

Vs.10: *"Your kingdom come, Your will be done on earth as it is in heaven."* - Spend time asking God, the Father, *what it is He wants to do* and *how He wants to do it*: in your life, our church, elsewhere;

Vs.11: *"Give us this day our daily bread."* - Spend time asking God, the Father, with confidence, for *your needs, the needs of our church, the needs of others*. Then *give thanks for what He has already provided!*

Vs.12: *"Forgive us our debts, as we also have forgiven our debtors."*

Spend time asking, God, the Father, how you are *indebted to Him* or *to someone else* by how you have sinned, (The word, *"debt"* implies how you have taken away from someone's *honor*; the word *forgive* means literally to *let go of*);

Then ask the Lord to *help you let go of your sin*. Ask the Lord to help you *let go of those who have sinned against you*, and have taken some of your honor away.

Vs.13: *"And do not lead us into temptation, but deliver us from evil."* - Close with asking God for His protection for you, for your family, for our church, for others. Then thank and praise Him for His goodness and grace.

"Praying for Vision"

1. Ask Jesus to show you the places, people and/or organizations the Spirit would have you speak to Jesus about on their behalf.

2. Ask Jesus to show you His heart for each. Then set up appointments with yourself throughout the coming week where, by faith, you will seek to "pray Jesus' heart" for them.

www.DennyFinnegan.com

LESSON 2: Foundation For All Our Ministry: "Intimacy With Jesus"

Laying a Biblical Foundation

How Jesus *"Kept the Main Thing the Main Thing!"*

Through the years, I've heard many whom I admire in the Kingdom of God make a common statement about ministry; that is, how important it is *"to keep the main thing the main thing!"*

When I think about how Jesus exemplified this - *"keeping the main thing the main thing"* - out of the many examples of what Jesus said, taught and did, there are two specific passages from the New Testament that continue to have a powerful impact upon my life:

> "35 *Jesus was going through all the cities and villages, teaching in their synagogues and proclaiming the gospel of the kingdom, and healing every kind of disease and every kind of sickness.* 36 *Seeing the people, He felt compassion for them, because they were distressed and dispirited like sheep without a shepherd.*"   (Matthew 9:35-36, NAS)

> "19 *Therefore Jesus answered and was saying to them, 'Truly, truly, I say to you, the Son can do nothing of Himself, unless it is something He sees the Father doing; for whatever the Father does, these things the Son also does in like manner.* 20 *For the*

Father loves the Son, and shows Him all things that He Himself is doing; and the Father will show Him greater works than these, so that you will marvel. "'
(John 5:19-20, NAS)

Matthew 9:35-36:

1. The Greek word for *"He felt compassion ..."* could literally translate as *"His guts ached ..."*

What was it about these people that stirred Jesus' *compassion*?

_____

_____

_____

_____

How does Jesus' *compassion* connect to Jesus mission and commission?

_____

_____

_____

How does Jesus' *compassion* in us connect to our mission and commission?

_____

_____

_____

_____

INTERCESSORY PRAYER MINI-COURSE

2. According to Matthew 9:35-36, *"What is the main thing"* to Jesus? How did Jesus *"keep the main thing the main thing"*?

_____

_____

_____

_____

John 5:19-20:

3. In this passage, Jesus describes "the source of His Mission and Commission."

How does Jesus describe His relationship with the Father?

_____

_____

_____

_____

What does that imply about our relationship with them?

_____

_____

_____

_____

_____

_____

How We Can *"Keep the Main Thing the Main Thing!*

Two more passages us for us to compare ...

> *"Love the LORD your God with all your heart and with all your soul and with all your strength."*

(Deuteronomy 6:5, NIV)

> *"We love, because He first loved us."* (1 John 4:19, NIV)

God does *not* ask anything *from us* that He has not already done *for us*!

1. How should this truth encourage us to pursue *God's love for us* and pursue *giving our love back to God*?

_____

_____

_____

2. How do these verses help us to stay focused in following Jesus?

_____

_____

_____

3. How do you let God love you? How do you respond in love to God?

_____

_____

16

Practicing What We Have Been Taught

Using Scripture to "pray and praise" has been one very "practical" and "helpful" personal discipline to draw closer to the heart of God, something I have been more intentional practicing and pursuing over the past 10+ years. For the next 20 minutes, each one of us is going to practice *letting God love us* and practice *giving our love back to God.*

Psalm 139:1-6:

1. Open up to Psalm 139:1-6. Find a place where you will not be distracted by others.

2. Ask the Holy Spirit to help you. Speak each verse to God as if they are *your own words* to God. After you speak each verse, stop and spend time thanking God as the Holy Spirit shows how it is *personally true for you.*

3. Journal what the Lord shows you.

4. Spend as much time as you need with each verse, even if you don't get past verse 1.

Praying for Vision

1. Find a prayer partner for this part of the lesson.

2. Ask Jesus to show you the places, people and/or organizations the Spirit would have you speak to Jesus about on their behalf. Ask Jesus to show you His heart for each.

3. "Debrief" with each other after you are finished praying for guidance and discuss how you can hold one another accountable for what you believe the Spirit is asking you to pray. Make sure you exchange phone numbers so you can talk during the week.

4. Then set up appointments with yourself throughout the coming week where, by faith, you will seek to "pray Jesus' heart" for what you were shown in #2. If possible, set up one or more appointments where you can pray together.

5. If you do *not* get a clear sense of anything, *that's okay ... it happens to me, too*! Persist in prayer for clarity during the week for yourself and for your prayer partner.

SECTION 2: "AN INTERCESSORY PRAYER MODEL"

LESSON 3: Praying by Listening
Part 1: "Honoring God" and
"Personal Cleansing"

LESSON 4: Praying by Listening
Part 2: "Dealing With The Enemy" and
"Personal Concerns"

LESSON 5: Praying by Listening
Part 3: "Meditate on the Word" and
"Pray What God Gives You"

LESSON 6: Praying by Listening
Part 4: "Persevering Prayer"

INTRODUCTION – An Intercessory Prayer Model

This *Intercessory Prayer Model* we are examining, in Section Two of this six week Bible Study, contains *seven elements* gleaned from many other Intercessory Prayer models, and also from many years of Intercessory Prayer experience - that of mine and that of others whom I respect. But all *seven elements* are solidly grounded in the Word of God.

While the presentation of these *seven elements* may imply a specific "order" for Intercession and Prayer, don't let yourself be limited by my suggestions. Our God is a creative God and is always active and intentional in all that He asks us to do, *even when He does not follow our/my suggested orders.* The *key principle* in all of prayer is, *"Praying by Listening"*. That means, while models may guide us and help us, God is, first and foremost, *our Help and Guide* (e.g., Psalm 43:3; 46:1). As you grow in your ability to listen to God, the Holy Spirit may creatively guide you to do something different than what is in this order, but just as effective (or more so).

When you are not sure what to do, quiet yourself before the Lord and *Listen to His Heart.* If you struggle in sensing God's guidance, as I do sometimes, then these *seven elements* may help you *jump-start* your prayer time. Always seek to be flexible; always seek to *listen.*

As an encouragement, here are three principles of prayer I have discovered as stated in the introduction to the *FOUNDATIONS: Prayer Ministry in the Local Church* Bible Study material:

1) *God's ability to communicate with us will always be greater than our inability to hear* - God is *not limited* by our ability when God wants to communicate with us.

2) *God's desire to communicate with us will always be stronger than whatever we may believe about God at any given moment* - God is *not deterred* by our lack of desire when God wants to relate to us.

3) *God's delight to communicate with us will always be 'immeasurably more than all we ask or imagine, according to His power that is at work within us'* (Ephesians 3:20) - God is *not disappointed* in us, because *God chose us* to be His children.

LESSON 3: Praying by Listening - Part 1: "Honoring God" and "Personal Cleansing"

The first 2 elements we will examine have to do with "our preparation" in *listening* to the Lord for when we intercede for ourselves or for others.

Laying a Biblical Foundation

A. "Honoring God"

> 1 *In the year that King Uzziah died, I saw the Lord seated on a throne, high and exalted, and the train of his robe filled the temple. 2 Above him were seraphs, each with six wings: With two wings they covered their faces, with two they covered their feet, and with two they were flying. 3 And they were calling to one another: "Holy, holy, holy is the LORD Almighty; the whole earth is full of his glory. 4 At the sound of their voices the doorposts and thresholds shook and the temple was filled with smoke.*

(Isaiah 6:1-3)

This heavenly vision that Isaiah received *came before* God gave a specific commission to Isaiah to mediate God's message to the people of those times, both Jew *and* Gentile. While this was a prophetic commission, it still connects with our basic definition for

23

Intercessory Prayer which is *"to intervene between parties with a view to reconciling differences; mediate"* (cf., with <u>Lesson #1</u>: *"What Is Intercessory Prayer"*).

1. It was God's decision to remind Isaiah of God's glory and honor before Isaiah represent God. Let's see what we learn of God's glory and how we might honor Him. In each verse, list and describe how God's glory and honor are described:

- <u>Vs.1:</u>

_____

_____

_____

- <u>Vs.2:</u>

_____

_____

_____

- <u>Vs.3:</u>

_____

_____

_____

- <u>Vs.4:</u>

_____

_____

_____

2. Why is it important to *glorify and honor* God before we seek to represent Him to others and others to Him?

_____

_____

_____

_____

B. "Personal Cleansing"

5 "Woe to me!" I cried. "I am ruined! For I am a man of unclean lips, and I live among a people of unclean lips, and my eyes have seen the King, the LORD Almighty." 6 Then one of the seraphs flew to me with a live coal in his hand, which he had taken with tongs from the altar. 7 With it he touched my mouth and said, "See, this has touched your lips; your guilt is taken away and your sin atoned for." 8 Then I heard the voice of the Lord saying, "Whom shall I send? And who will go for us?" And I said, "Here am I. Send me!" (Isaiah 6:5-8)

14 Therefore, since we have a great high priest who has gone through the heavens, Jesus the Son of God, let us hold firmly to the faith we profess. 15 For we do not have a high priest who is unable to sympathize with our weaknesses, but we have one who has been tempted in every way, just as we are-- yet was without sin. 16 Let us then approach the throne of grace with confidence, so that we may receive mercy and find grace to help us in our time of need. (Hebrews 4:14-16)

These next four verses in Isaiah 6 reveal to us Isaiah's *awareness* of what it means to represent God. But we also live under the New Covenant with Jesus acting as both our High Priest and Mediator/Intercessor before the Father's throne. These two passages reveal both *our need* and *our hope!*

1. What do these two passages say about *our need* when we intercede?

_____

_____

_____

_____

2. What do these two passages say about *our hope* when we intercede?

_____

_____

_____

_____

Practicing What We Have Been Taught

You don't have to complete everything in this section of the lesson! The important thing is to let yourself be lead by the Holy Spirit and allow God to be *your help* and *your guide* (confer with Psalm 43:3; 46:1). You can always come back and finish this part of the lesson at another time.

"Honoring God"

1. Spend time reflectively praying over Isaiah 6:1-4. Enter into a time of *glorifying* and *honoring* with the words of the text, or with your own words of honor and exaltation. Stay with this part of the lesson as long as you sense the Holy Spirit leading you to do so. (Make time after the lesson is over to journal what the Lord showed you about His glory and honor).

"Personal Cleansing"

2. As you sense the Holy Spirit leading you, begin to reflectively pray over Isaiah 6:5-7 and Hebrews 4:14-16. Allow the Holy Spirit to show you any particular areas of "cleansing" that Jesus wants to bring to you. (Make time after the lesson is over to journal what the Lord showed you about His cleansing of you).

"Praying for Vision"

3. As you sense the Holy Spirit leading you, begin to reflectively pray over Isaiah 6:8.

Ask Jesus to show you how *His cleansing of you* is connected to *His preparation of you* to serve Him. Write it down.

_____

_____

_____

_____

_____

      Now, repeat Isaiah's words as if they are also your own.

How and ***for whom*** **is Jesus calling you** to *represent* in prayer? Write it down.

_____

_____

_____

_____

_____

Where **is Jesus sending you to *represent* Him?** Write it down.

_____

_____

_____

_____

_____

LESSON 4: Praying by Listening - Part 2: "Dealing With The Enemy" and "Personal Concerns"

The next 2 elements we will examine have to do with "clearing away the distractions" in *listening* to the Lord for when we intercede for ourselves or for others. It would be very easy to reverse these two elements with those of the previous lesson. But I have found that these two - *"Dealing with the Enemy"* and *"Personal Concerns"* - are dealt with easier when we let God's grace and power go before us, just like the people of Israel marched into the Promised Land and into God's Promises with the ark of covenant before them.

But remember to be flexible and let God arrange your prayer time for you.

Laying a Biblical Foundation

A. "Dealing with the Enemy"

> "1 *Listen to my prayer, O God, do not ignore my plea; 2 hear me and answer me. My thoughts trouble me and I am distraught 3 at the voice of the enemy, at the stares of the wicked; for they bring down suffering upon me and revile me in their anger.*" (Psalm 55:1-3)

Our enemies may come in all shapes and sizes and types, including those "unseen" (cf. Ephesians 6:10-

29

13), and even those who we thought were our friends (cf. Psalm 55:12-14). Whatever or "whoever" the source, *enemies* can be a definite distraction to God's call to represent Him to others and others to Him in prayer.

1. Lets look at Psalm 55:1-9, to see how David was affected by his enemies. List the words and phrases that describe *what* his enemies were doing, and *how* it distracted David:

<u>Vs.1-3:</u>

_____

_____

_____

_____

<u>Vs.4-6:</u>

_____

_____

_____

_____

<u>Vs.5-7:</u>

_____

_____

_____

_____

2. Lets look at Psalm 55:16-18 and **Ephesians 6:10-13,18** for our solution to *Dealing with the Enemy*. In each passage, list *what we give to God* and *what God gives to us*:

Psalm 55:16-18:

_____

_____

_____

_____

Ephesians 6:10-13,18:

_____

_____

_____

_____

B. "Personal Concerns"

> "*22 Cast your cares on the LORD and he will
> sustain you; he will never let the righteous fall.
> 23 But you, O God, will bring down the wicked
> into the pit of corruption; bloodthirsty and
> deceitful men will not live out half their days. But
> as for me, I trust in you.*" (Psalm 55:22-23)

From the study we have done in Psalm 55 so far,
we have a good picture of how the enemy, both "seen"
and "unseen" may come against us. The Hebrew word
David uses for "cares", literally translates as "what has
been given or provided; gift". To help us hear the voice
of the Lord better, it is good to know how to remove
these "unwanted gifts" as distractions to our call to
intercede, whether from enemies or the "cares of the
world."

1. Let's see how David dealt with the distractions of
"what was given" to him that also applies to "what life

may give us". In each verse, list *what we give to God* and *what God gives to us*:

Vs.22:

_____

_____

_____

Vs.23:

_____

_____

_____

_____

2. **Summarize:** What have you learned in this lesson about *Dealing with the Enemy* and *Personal Concerns* from Psalm 55 and Ephesians 6:10-13,18.

_____

_____

_____

_____

_____

_____

_____

_____

_____

_____

_____

Practicing What We Have Been Taught

You don't have to complete everything in this section of the lesson! The important thing is to let yourself be lead by the Holy Spirit and allow God to be *your help* and *your guide* (confer with Psalm 43:3; 46:1). You can always come back and finish this part of the lesson at another time.

"Dealing with the Enemy"

1 Listen to my prayer, O God, do not ignore my plea; 2 hear me and answer me. My thoughts trouble me and I am distraught 3 at the voice of the enemy ...

1. In the table below, in the left column, make a list of some of the ways you currently feel "troubled" or "distraught"; in the right column, ask the Holy Spirit to help you discern the possible source(s) of each. These are "cares" that have the potential to distract or discourage you in hearing the Lord's voice as you intercede.

As you do this second part, it is important to remember that the Holy Spirit will *not* accuse, condemn or belittle you, just reveal so that we may be able to move toward a solution of freedom in the power of Christ!

33

What is Distraught and Troubled in My Life	Source

"Personal Concerns"

22 Cast your cares on the LORD and he will sustain you; he will never let the righteous fall. 23 ... But as for me, I trust in you.

2. In the left column, ask the Holy Spirit to reveal to you *how* to "cast off" these distractions and disconnect their sources from you; in the right column, ask the Holy Spirit to reveal *how* you need to trust Jesus for each.

It may not be real complicated for each. But if you sense something "blocking" you from releasing a care to Christ, get together with some other brothers or sisters in the Lord at a later time and ask them to pray with you and help you discern the source of "the block" together. If you find it necessary to pray with others for "blocks", remember to stand in Christ' victory and love for you, not your sense of defeat or failure.

Because of Christ's victory for us at the cross, *we do not have to be perfect* before we can effectively hear the Lord or effectively pray.

How to Cast Off Each Distraction	*How* I Am Called to Trust Jesus

Praying for Vision

3. As you sense the Holy Spirit leading you, begin to reflectively pray over Psalm 55:22-23. Repeat David's words as if they are your own.

Ask Jesus to show you how *His releasing of you* is connected to *His preparation of you* to serve Him. Write it down.

_____

_____

_____

_____

How and *for whom* **is Jesus calling you** to *represent* in prayer? Write it down.

_____
_____
_____
_____
_____
_____
_____
_____

Where **is Jesus sending you to** *represent* **Him?** Write it down.

_____
_____
_____
_____

LESSON 5 : Praying by Listening - Part 3: - "Meditate on the Word" and "Pray What God Gives You"

Knowing what to pray for someone can be difficult at times. This is where I have seen a strong connection between my time in *deep reflection in the Word of God* and *the Lord's guidance in what to pray.* For "deep reflection" is part of the heart of the meaning for the word "meditate", just as "meditation upon the Word of God" is an important part of God's Heart when we seek to pray His heart for others through intercessory prayer.

For this lesson, I am going to use two of the Apostle Paul's prayers for the people of Ephesus to demonstrate how letting the Holy Spirit speak to us through the Word of God can also offer the Holy Spirit the opportunity to reveal to us how we can pray God's Heart for others.

Laying a Biblical Foundation

A. **"Meditate on the Word"**

Open up your bibles to each passage, *reflect deeply* on each passage, and make a list of the various things Paul prays for the Ephesians.

Ephesians 1:15-23   **Ephesians 3:14-21**

B. "Pray What God Gives You"

Under each column, write down what you sense were the specific needs the Holy Spirit was showing Paul to pray for the Ephesians.

Ephesians 1:15-23   **Ephesians 3:14-21**

Practicing What We Have Been Taught and Praying for Vision

You don't have to complete everything in this section of the lesson! The important thing is to let yourself be lead by the Holy Spirit and allow God to be *your help* and *your guide* (confer with Psalm 43:3; 46:1). You can always come back and finish this part of the lesson at another time.

"Meditate on the Word" and "Pray What God Gives You"

We are going to combine and practice both of these sections together. In the left column, ask the Holy Spirit for the names, communities or nations that are upon Jesus' Heart at this moment, those whom Jesus would have you present to Him and He to them in prayer. In the right column, ask the Holy Spirit to show you what from Paul's prayers Jesus would have your pray for them.

WHO Is On Jesus' Heart	*WHAT* Is On Jesus' Heart for Them

LESSON 6 : Praying by Listening - Part 4: - "Persevering Prayer"

As we wrap up this short course on Intercessory Prayer, we look at an element that is often *overlooked* by many of us - that of "perseverance" in our prayer-intercessions; that of "staying the course" until we sense permission from the Holy Spirit to stop. In *Persevering Prayer*, the burden to pray for someone or something may last only a few moments a day, over the course of several days, several weeks, or maybe even several years; or it might be a travailing work that lasts an hour or more as a continuous "birthing process" for something God is about to do, then just simply stops.

Whatever way the Holy Spirit might manifest this call to intercession, I would like to assure you of two things: 1) the Lord will *never* expose us to anything that He knows we are incapable of handling *in Him* (cf. 1 Corinthians 10:13); and, 2) we are capable to do this type of intercession, because it is God's power that is as work within us and through us, not our own (cf. 2 Corinthians 4:7).

To give us a better idea of the kind of character God wants to develop within us to be called to this kind of prayer, we are going to look at "the concept of perseverance", then some "snapshots" of "perseverance" within scripture as we apply it to our understanding of *Persevering Prayer*.

A. The Concept of *Perseverance.*

> 10 *Finally, be strong in the Lord and in his mighty power.* 11 *Put on the full armor of God so that you can take your stand against the devil's schemes.* 12 *For our struggle is not against flesh and blood, but against the rulers, against the authorities, against the powers of this dark world and against the spiritual forces of evil in the heavenly realms.* 13 *Therefore put on the full armor of God, so that when the day of evil comes, you may be able to stand your ground, and after you have done everything, to stand...* 18 *And pray in the Spirit on all occasions with all kinds of prayers and requests. With this in mind, be alert and always keep on praying for all the saints.*

(Ephesians 6:10-13,18)

1. In Ephesians 6:10-13, the Apostle Paul describes our role in the advancement of the Kingdom of God as being like a "warrior" in battle. And in Ephesians 6:18, the Apostle Paul connects *"our struggle"* to *"our persevering prayer"*.

What does God supply for the battle and why?

_____

_____

_____

_____

_____

How do we cooperate with God in this battle?

_____

_____

_____

Where is perseverance and endurance necessary and why?

_____

_____

_____

_____

2. In Ephesians 4:12, the Greek word for "struggle", literally translates as "wrestle", and the Hebrew equivalent, where " *a man **wrestled** with*" Jacob in Genesis 32:24-26, means "get dusty, dust."

> 24 *So Jacob was left alone, and a man **wrestled** with him till daybreak.* 25 *When the man saw that he could not overpower him, he touched the socket of Jacob's hip so that his hip was wrenched as he **wrestled** with the man.* 26 *Then the man said, "Let me go, for it is daybreak." But Jacob replied, "I will not let you go unless you bless me."*
> Genesis 32:24-26

It may require us to get "sweaty and dirty" in order to "reach the blessing" God has in mind through our prayers!

What does it require to "wrestle?" To "wrestle in prayer?"

_____

_____

_____

_____

When was a time the Lord had you "wrestle in your prayer" for someone or something?

_____

_____

_____

B. Three "Snapshots" of *Perseverance*.

> 8 *These are the names of David's mighty men: Josheb-Basshebeth, a Tahkemonite, was chief of the Three; he raised his spear against eight hundred men, whom he killed in one encounter.* 9 *Next to him was Eleazar son of Dodai the Ahohite. As one of the three mighty men, he was with David when they taunted the Philistines gathered at Pas Dammim for battle. Then the men of Israel retreated,* 10 *but he stood his ground and struck down the Philistines till his hand grew tired and froze to the sword. The LORD brought about a great victory that day. The troops returned to Eleazar, but only to strip the dead.* 11 *Next to him was Shammah son of Agee the Hararite. When the Philistines banded together at a place where there was a field full of lentils, Israel's troops fled from them.* 12 *But Shammah took his stand in the middle of the field. He defended it and struck the Philistines down, and the LORD brought about a great victory.*
> (2 Samuel 23:8-12)

Each of these men were mighty warriors. The way each of these men battled can give us a better understanding of what *Persevering Prayer* might look like for us, as led by the Holy Spirit. Look at what each these *"three mighty men of David"* did, then apply what you learn to persevering prayer.

1. *Josheb-Basshebeth, a Tahkemonite* (vs.8):

_____

_____

_____

_____

_____

2. *Eleazar son of Dodai the Ahohite* (vs.9-10):

_____

_____

_____

_____

_____

3. *Shammah son of Agee the Hararite* (vs.11-12):

_____

_____

_____

_____

_____

Practicing What We Have Been Taught and Praying for Vision

We are going to combine "practice" and "vision" together. It will be based upon what you prayed in the last lesson. You don't have to complete everything in this section of the lesson! The important thing is to let yourself be lead by the Holy Spirit and allow God to be *your help* and *your guide* (confer with Psalm 43:3; 46:1). You can always come back and finish this part of the lesson at another time.

"Persevering Prayer"

In the left column, ask the Holy Spirit who are the names, the communities or nations from the last lesson that are still upon Jesus' Heart this week. In the right column, ask the Holy Spirit to show you *how* you are to continue to battle for them and "wrestle for the blessing" God has appointed for them.

WHO Is On Jesus' Heart	*WHAT* Is On Jesus' Heart for Them

PRAYER JOURNAL

Date: Need: Date Answered:

_____

_____

_____

_____

_____

_____

_____

_____

_____

_____

_____

_____

_____

_____

_____

_____

_____

_____

_____

_____

_____

_____

_____

_____

_____

_____

ABOUT THE AUTHOR

Rev. Denny Finnegan is a spirit-filled ordained minister who has 30 years of full-time practical ministerial experience, and 5 years part-time experience. He loves to help people grow in their relationship with Jesus Christ, and to help them be more effective in their witness for Jesus through how they serve Him and serve others.

DENNY FINNEGAN'S OTHER WORKBOOKS

FOUNDATIONS : Understanding Prayer Ministry
Prayer Ministry in the Local Church
ISBN: 978-0-615-34744-8   52895
Excellent Adventures! Inc. Press

Foundation Series:
Intercessory Prayer Mini-Course
Growing Personally As An Intercessor
ISBN: 978-0-9889584-3-2
Available on Amazon as a Kindle Book

Foundation Series:
Healing Prayer Mini-Course
Living the Healing Ministry of Jesus
ISBN: 978-0-9889584-2-5
Available on Amazon as a Kindle Book

Foundation Series:
Prophetic Prayer Mini-Course
Living a Prophetic Lifestyle
ISBN: 978-0-9889584-1-8
Available on Amazon as a Kindle Book